Whodunit?

Whodunit?

Science Solves the Crime

Steven Otfinoski

illustrated by

Betsy Scheld

Scientific American Books for Young Readers

W. H. Freeman and Company / New York

Book design by Richard Oriolo

Scientific American Books for Young Readers is an imprint of
W. H. Freeman and Company, 41 Madison Avenue, New York, NY 10010.

Library of Congress Cataloging-in-Publication Data

Otfinoski, Steven.
Whodunit? : science solves the crime / Steven Otfinoski ;
illustrated by Betsy Scheld.
p. cm. — (Scientific American mysteries of science)
Summary: Uses ten actual cases to show how science is used to investigate and solve crimes.
ISBN 0-7167-6515-2 (alk. paper). — ISBN 0-7167-6559-4 (pbk. : alk.paper)
1. Forensic sciences—Case studies—Juvenile literature. 2. Crime investigation—Case studies—Juvenile literature. [1. Forensic sciences. 2. Criminal investigation.] I. Scheld, Betsy, ill. II. Title. III. Series.
HV8073.8.086 1995 95-11961
363.2'5—dc20 CIP
AC

Printed in the United States of America

10 9 8 7 6 5 4 3 2 1

Contents

Introduction

A crime has been committed. The criminal must be brought to justice. But how?

For most of human history, this question was not easy to answer. If no one actually saw a person commit a crime, or if the person left behind no obvious clues, authorities had no way to connect the criminal to the crime. So what did they do?

Often they turned to torture and superstition to get a suspect to confess. One kind of superstitious "trial" involved throwing an accused person into a body of water. If the person floated, the verdict was guilty. If the person sank, the verdict was not guilty. Small comfort for the innocent!

Only in the last 200 years or so has crime detection become effective, thanks largely to modern science. As technology has forged ahead, crime fighters have

found ways of using it to help solve such age-old crimes as murder, robbery, and forgery.

An entire branch of science has developed that deals with crime detection. It is called forensic science. *Forensic* comes from a Latin word, *forensis,* that means "forum"—court of law. The evidence forensic scientists discover and carefully analyze is used in courts of law to convict criminals.

The ten true crime cases you will read about in this book cover some of the highlights in the history of forensic science up to the present. Each case deals with one important aspect of forensics, including fingerprinting, ballistics (guns and bullets), the detection of gases and poisons, the analysis of blood and body tissue, and

DNA fingerprinting. The crimes you will read about range from art forgery to drug smuggling to murder—and you should be warned: some of them are fairly grisly. Along the way you'll meet some of the most persistent science detectives in the world—from a master-criminal-turned-police-inspector in Paris, France, to a drug-sniffing cocker spaniel in Miami, Florida.

So settle back in your chair, put up your feet, and find out how science has helped answer that burning question: Whodunit?

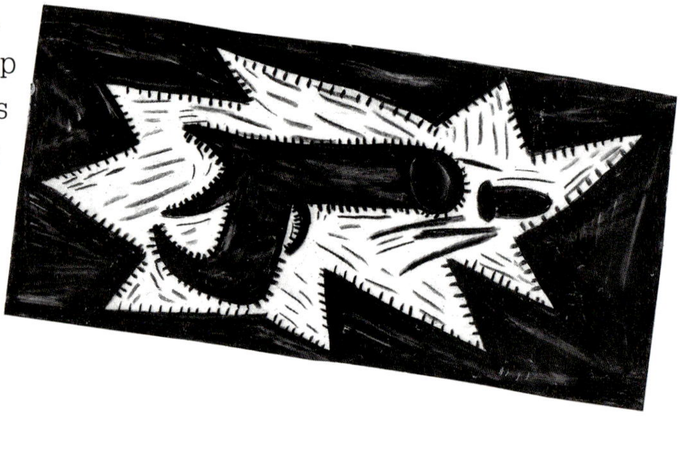

Chapter 1

The Butcher, the Thieves, and the Wolf

The butcher Fontaine was not by nature a nervous man. But the rash of violent robberies near Paris, France, that fall of 1821 had him worried. Heading home to Courtille from a harvest fair, he was carrying 1,500 francs in his purse—a considerable amount of money in those days.

Fontaine was relieved when he met three well-dressed gentlemen at the roadside inn where he stopped for an evening meal. They too were headed for Courtille, and they suggested to Fontaine that the four of them complete the journey together, for safety's sake.

Later that evening, they left the inn. Soon the

four men were walking single file down a narrow lane in the darkness. Without warning, the man behind Fontaine clubbed him on the back of the head. As the butcher staggered forward, another of his companions pulled out a knife. Fontaine was a large man, and he did not give up his purse without a fight. But the three robbers attacked him savagely. At last he collapsed with twenty-eight stab wounds. The "gentlemen" took his purse and left him bleeding in the lane.

Fortunately, another traveler found Fontaine and took him to the nearest hospital. The butcher miraculously survived. One of Fontaine's first visitors was the local prosecutor, who questioned him about the brutal attack.

Fontaine gave the prosecutor a full description of the three men who had robbed and beaten him. Local police scoured the scene of the crime for clues. They found some buttons, cloth fragments, and a bloodstained scrap of paper that one of the thieves must have dropped.

The prosecutor turned these clues over to François Eugène Vidocq, the chief of the Paris police force, known as the Sûreté. Vidocq's sharp mind searched for method and order in criminal activities. He saw a similar pattern between this robbery and others in the area. He had a hunch that the same men were responsible for all these attacks. But who were they?

Examining all the clues, Vidocq focused his attention on the bloody scrap of paper. He studied it for a long, long time. He came to the conclusion that the writing on it was part of an address. He recognized the address as that of a local wine merchant named Clair Raoul. Besides wine, Raoul's shop was often filled with shady characters, who used it as a meeting place.

Vidocq moved slowly but surely. Once the police chief smelled the scent of a criminal, he would not rest until he had hunted him down. That is how he earned his nickname, "The Wolf."

Vidocq ordered some of his agents to stake out Raoul's wine shop. He knew that Raoul's neighbors could tell him many things about the shopkeeper's activities. But he also knew that these people didn't trust the police or were afraid to be seen talking to them. So he had his men disguise themselves as petty criminals. This wasn't difficult, because every one of his agents had formerly lived a life of crime. Vidocq felt that the best person to catch a crook was another crook.

The neighbors weren't suspicious of the disguised agents and talked openly to them. Vidocq learned some interesting facts about Clair Raoul. Late at night, two men, dirty with the dust of the road, regularly visited Raoul's shop. The appearance of one of the men matched Fontaine's description of one of his attackers. Vidocq recognized the man as he saw him leave Raoul's shop. He was Monsieur Court, a thief Vidocq had arrested once before. The police chief immediately ordered several men to follow Court.

Court's behavior was suspicious. He slept during the day and went out at night. He seemed to have no regular job, but he always had plenty of money to spend. Vidocq had seen enough. He got a warrant and personally arrested Court.

With Court in jail, Vidocq now went after Raoul. The wine merchant was clever, and Vidocq knew he would have to be even more clever to catch him. He did not accuse Raoul of dealing with criminals. He did not want to arouse his suspicions and perhaps cause him to flee. Instead, he accused Raoul of harboring political dissenters who met in his shop and sang songs disloyal to the republic. When Raoul denied the charge, Vidocq had his shop searched for copies of the songs. He was really looking for evidence to connect Raoul to the robberies. The search turned up nothing. Vidocq then accompanied Raoul home to search his house.

Again, the search seemed futile—until a policeman found a document in a drawer. When he showed it to Vidocq, the police chief's eyes grew wide as he read. A corner of the document that had contained Raoul's address was torn off. Vidocq took out the scrap of paper found at the scene of the crime. It matched the missing corner perfectly. Now Vidocq had solid proof that Raoul was somehow involved in the robbery.

Raoul lunged toward a brace of pistols, but two Sûreté agents grabbed him. The shopkeeper refused to speak another word.

Soon after Raoul was jailed, Vidocq had Court brought out of his cell. The police chief began to question him, not mentioning of what crime he was being accused. Nervous and unsure of what would happen next, Court broke down and confessed to the robbery and murder of a poultry dealer. Vidocq hid his surprise and asked about the robbery of the butcher. Court admitted that he and Raoul had committed that robbery too. He assumed Fontaine was dead, but Vidocq assured him that he was still alive. The two men were brought before Fontaine, who identified them both. Later, a third man was arrested for the robbery.

Justice for Court and Raoul was swift. They were tried, convicted, and condemned to be beheaded for the murder of the poultry dealer.

On the day of the execution, the butcher Fontaine showed up to heckle his attackers as they stood before the guillotine. Vidocq ordered Fontaine to be removed from the place of execution. He felt the two men should die with dignity.

The policeman's behavior may have puzzled some of the crowd watching the execution. But the men of the Sûreté were not surprised. They knew that, like themselves, the greatest detective in all of France had once himself been a notorious criminal. The Wolf had not forgotten what it felt like to be the hunted.

François Eugène Vidocq's life is as exciting as any adventure story. In fact, he has turned up as a fictitious character in several novels, including some by his good friend the famous novelist Honoré Balzac. Born in 1775, Vidocq ran away from home and joined the army at age 15. At 18 he married, but shortly afterward found his wife was having an affair with an army officer. Vidocq beat the officer and was thrown in jail. He escaped and embarked on a life of crime. He was arrested many times but always managed to escape. To elude capture, Vidocq became a master of disguise, impersonating all kinds of people from a doctor to a nun!

Tired of his life of crime, Vidocq eventually turned himself in to the police and offered to serve as an informer. The Paris police felt Vidocq's knowledge of the criminal world would be invaluable. He eventually became the head of the Brigade de Sûreté, the world's first modern police force. He developed the first criminal files, keeping records of criminals' physical appearances, the kinds of crimes they committed, and their methods of working.

In the Fontaine case, Vidocq used a number of investigative methods that are still used by police around the world today: victims' descriptions, undercover investigation, stakeouts, house searches, corroborating evidence, past criminal patterns, and psychological methods in the questioning of a suspect.

Chapter 2

Mark of a Killer

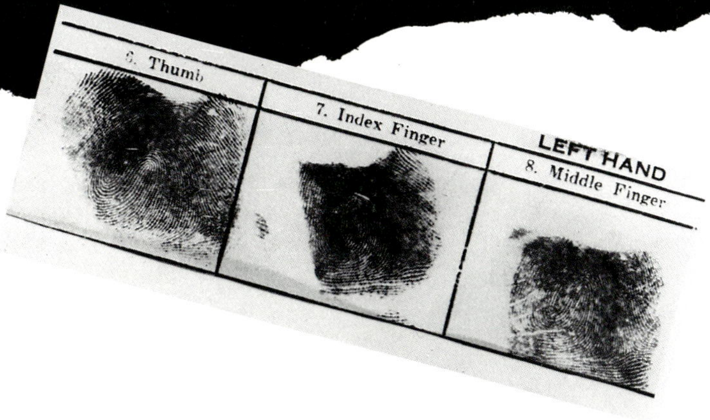

On the evening of June 19, 1892, two young children were found by their mother battered to death in their bedroom in Necochea, Argentina. It was a particularly brutal murder, even by big-city standards. That it had happened in a tiny village on the Atlantic coast was more shocking.

The mother, Francisca Rojas, claimed to have been returning home from work when she saw a neighbor, an old man named Velasquez, fleeing from her hut. She told the police that earlier in the day Velasquez had asked her to marry him. When she had refused, she reported, he had sworn he would kill what she loved most.

But Velasquez had an alibi. Another neighbor, who lived a mile away from the Rojas home, claimed that Velasquez had been visiting him.

All the same, the local police chief had Velasquez arrested and beaten to try

to obtain a confession. But the old man insisted he was innocent.

The chief then heard a rumor that shifted suspicion to Francisca Rojas. Neighbors gossiped that she was in love with a younger man who wouldn't marry her because of her children. Had love for this man led her to murder her own children?

The police chief tried to frighten Rojas into confessing. He stood outside her window at night and cried that he was the avenging spirit of her dead children. But

Rojas didn't budge. She either knew it was a trick or was actually innocent. The next morning she denied any involvement in her children's deaths.

The police chief didn't know whom to believe. What would he do? He decided to send to La Plata, the nearest large city, for help. La Plata police inspector Alvarez arrived to take over the investigation.

How were Alvarez's methods different from the local police chief's? Alvarez would not resort to violence or superstition to unmask the murderer. He was one of a small breed of detectives who used science and his own instincts to solve crime. Alvarez questioned both the suspect and his accuser. Then he visited the scene of the crime.

The two-room shack still bore the signs of the murder. Dried blood was matted on the bedsheets where the victims had lain. The inspector's eyes traveled around the room and came to rest on the door. There was a bloody thumbprint on it. The killer had undoubtedly left it as he—or she—dashed out of the house.

To another detective, the thumbprint would have meant nothing. In 1892, fingerprints were little understood as clues in criminal cases. But to Alvarez it was an important piece of evidence. He looked closely at the print. Its swirling lines were distinct and clear. Alvarez became excited. He turned to the local police chief, who had accompanied him, and asked for a saw. The chief shook his head as the inspector sawed off the section of the door containing the thumbprint. Alvarez's action made no sense to him. Most of the police inspectors back in La Plata would have shared the chief's feelings.

Alvarez, however, was convinced that he was onto something as he headed back to the police station with the piece of door. Some months earlier, he'd met Juan Vucetich, a police researcher. Vucetich, like Alvarez, was something of a maverick. He had been hired by the government of Argentina to introduce to the police department of every major city a new system that used criminals' body measurements for identification. But Vucetich had read in a science journal about a system of identification that he felt was more reliable—fingerprinting. He developed his own fingerprinting system and introduced it to the various police departments.

Most of the detectives had listened politely as Vucetich presented his system. But they were skeptical. Inspector Alvarez was one of the few detectives who weren't. Now, in the tiny village of Necochea, Alvarez was about to put Vucetich's theories to the test.

Back at the station, Alvarez studied the bloody thumbprint carefully with a magnifying glass. He noted the intricate pattern of swirls and whorls. Then he had

Velasquez and Rojas brought in. He asked Velasquez to place each thumb on an ink pad and make a print on a piece of paper. The inspector then held the paper alongside the thumbprint on the door and compared them. The prints didn't match.

Rojas started to protest. But Alvarez quietly asked her to place her thumbs on the ink pad. She was surprised and asked why. The inspector only repeated his request, quietly but firmly. The woman looked at the blank faces of the police officers who stood nearby and realized she had no choice. She made her thumbprints on the paper, and Alvarez compared them with the print on the door. Rojas's right thumbprint was a perfect match with the killer's print.

Confronted with the evidence, Francisca Rojas broke down and confessed. She *had* killed her children so her lover would marry her. While they slept, she had struck them with a rock, which she had then thrown into a well.

The local police chief shook his head. Maybe there was something to these fingerprints after all!

The Necochea case was the talk of Argentina. Alvarez had proved that Vucetich's classification of fingerprints could capture criminals more effectively than any other method. Argentina soon became the first country in the world to use fingerprinting as standard police procedure in criminal investigations. Other South American countries followed. By the second decade of the twentieth century, fingerprinting was being used as well by police in Europe and the United States.

The system of identification that Juan Vucetich replaced with fingerprinting was developed by Alphonse Bertillon, who worked at the Paris Sûreté after Vidocq's time. Convicts' heads, fingers, and arms were carefully measured, recorded, and kept on file. Bertillon calculated that with 14 measurements, the odds against two people having the same measurements were 286,435,456 to 1.

But Bertillon's system wasn't foolproof. The measurements could be slightly different, depending on who was taking them.

Fingerprints, the unique patterns on the skin of a person's fingertips, had been known and appreciated for centuries. Chinese emperors had used thumbprints as signatures on important documents. Yet it wasn't until the 1860s that anyone thought about using fingerprints to solve crimes.

William James Herschel was a government worker in India, at that time a British colony. To prevent retired people from trying to collect their pension more than once each month and also to prevent impostors from taking the

945

money, Herschel looked for an exact means of identification. He had all pensioners make their fingerprints on paper when collecting their money. One month he caught an imposter whose fingerprints didn't match the earlier set.

Dr. Henry Faulds, another Englishman who worked in a Japanese hospital, shared Herschel's interest in fingerprints. When two sooty handprints were found at the scene of a robbery, Faulds compared them with the prints of a man accused of the theft. The prints didn't match, and the man was released. Another suspect's prints did match the handprints, and that man was convicted of the crime. It was the first crime solved using fingerprints.

Today the FBI fingerprint file in Washington, D.C., one of the world's largest, contains millions of prints. The prints are computerized, and a particular print can be found in a matter of minutes. According to experts, the chance of two people having identical prints would occur only once in 4,660,377 centuries!

Chapter 3

The Bullets That Saved a Life

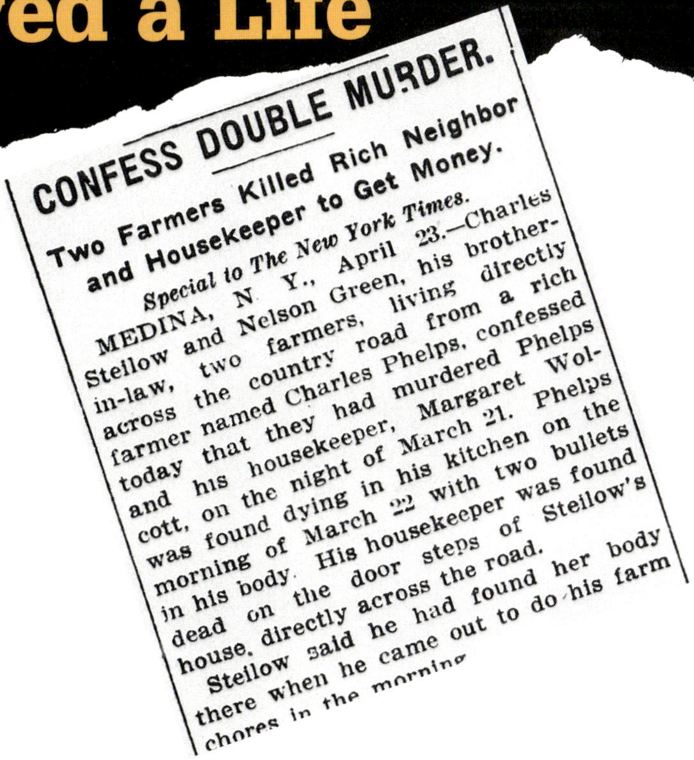

CONFESS DOUBLE MURDER.

Two Farmers Killed Rich Neighbor and Housekeeper to Get Money.

Special to The New York Times.

MEDINA, N. Y., April 23.—Charles Stellow and Nelson Green, his brother-in-law, two farmers, living directly across the country road from a rich farmer named Charles Phelps, confessed today that they had murdered Phelps and his housekeeper, Margaret Wolcott, on the night of March 21. Phelps was found dying in his kitchen on the morning of March 22 with two bullets in his body. His housekeeper was found dead on the door steps of Stellow's house, directly across the road. Stellow said he had found her body there when he came out to do his farm chores in the morning

West Shelby township in Orleans County in upstate New York was a quiet farming community, where even minor crimes were rarely committed. So, on a cold morning in March of 1915, when word spread of a double murder out at the Phelps farm, the incident had the whole town talking.

Sheriff Chester Bartlett had been summoned to the crime scene by Nelson Green, a hired hand at the Phelps place. Green was not particularly clear in his report, and it was only when the sheriff arrived at the scene and talked with Green's brother-in-law, Charles E. Stielow, that he got the full story. Earlier that morning, Stielow, who also worked for Phelps, had discovered the bloodied body of Margaret Wolcott, Phelps's housekeeper, on his doorstep. Nearby, in the main house, he had found his boss, seventy-year-old Charles Phelps, lying in a pool of blood with three bullets in him. Phelps had been taken to a hospital but died there without regaining consciousness.

The motive for the murders was clearly robbery. Phelps's desk had been broken into and all the money taken. But Sheriff Bartlett had never investigated a murder case before, and he made a serious error. He didn't immediately seal off the murder site to the public. Neighbors and curiosity seekers trampled through the Phelps property, destroying any clues. The sheriff brought in a bloodhound, but the frozen ground offered no scent to follow. The only evidence Bartlett had were the three bullets doctors removed from Phelps's body. They were fired from a .22 caliber revolver.

At the coroner's inquest a few days later, both Stielow and Green denied owning a .22 caliber gun or any gun at all. Sheriff Bartlett was stumped. What did he do? What many law enforcement officers at that time did when faced with a baffling crime. He hired a private detective.

This detective, named Newton, was no Sherlock Holmes. His method of solving a crime was to find a likely suspect and somehow force a confession from him. The mostly likely candidate was weak-willed Nelson Green. So Newton had Green arrested on suspicion of murder. In a short time the detective frightened Green into admitting that Stielow had lied about not owning any firearms. Green said Stielow had him hide three weapons—a revolver, a shotgun, and a rifle. All three were .22 caliber. Before the night was over, Green had confessed to helping Stielow murder Phelps and Wolcott in a botched robbery.

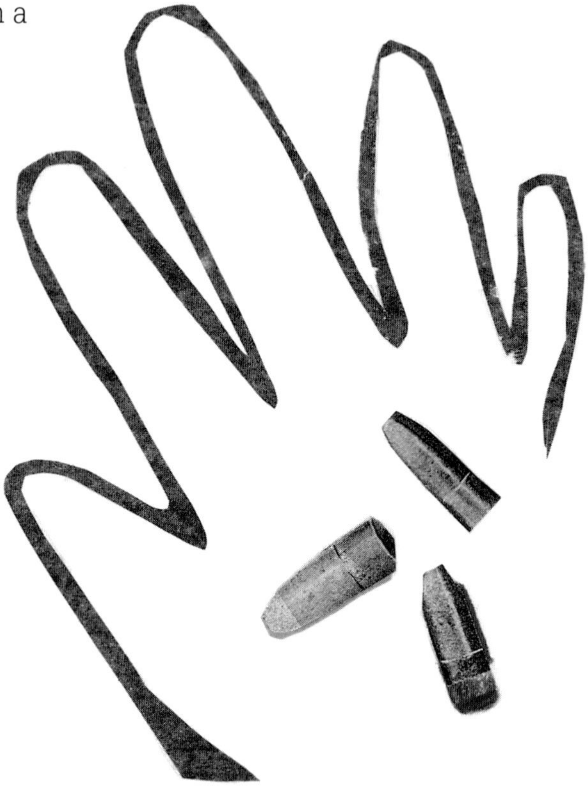

Stielow was not as easily intimidated as his brother-in-law. Under questioning, he admitted he had lied about the guns out of fear but denied he had killed anyone. Bartlett and Newton continued to question Stielow for two days. During that time he was allowed no food or sleep. Tired and depressed, Stielow confessed to the murders just so he could go home and see his pregnant wife.

The people of Orleans County wanted to get the murder trial over with as quickly as possible. A long trial would be expensive and bring unwanted publicity. However, even the judge

thought Stielow's "confession," which he denied in court, was suspect. It left a number of questions unanswered. Why had the housekeeper fled to the killers' cottage after the attack? Why would Stielow have left her body on his doorstep and then gone to sleep? And why had none of the stolen money turned up?

The case against Stielow looked weak, but the prosecutor had an ace up his sleeve. He brought in an "expert witness" to testify against the accused. "Dr." Albert Hamilton called himself a pioneer in the new field of forensic science. In truth, Hamilton's only experience in science was as a manufacturer of patent medicines. But his courtroom manner was so impressive that, based on his questionable testimony, juries in many criminal cases had found defendants guilty.

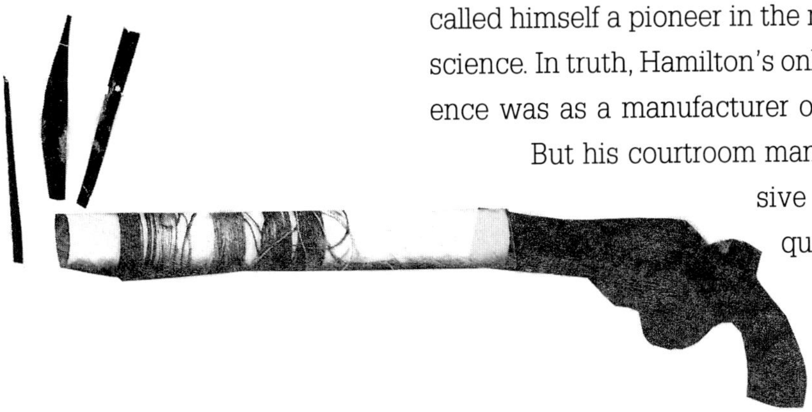

Hamilton showed the jury Stielow's revolver and several large photographs he had taken of the bullets that killed Phelps. He claimed to have found an "abnormal scratch" near the gun's muzzle and similar scratches on the bullets. Although the muzzle was an unusual place to find firing marks, Hamilton explained that the cartridge fit so tightly into the gun's barrel that no explosive gases could escape to the rear section of the barrel.

When Stielow's lawyer pointed out that there were no scratch marks on the bullets in the photos, Hamilton explained that he had merely photographed the wrong sides of the bullets.

The jury accepted Hamilton's testimony without question. Stielow was found guilty of first-degree murder and sent to New York's Sing Sing prison to await execution in the electric chair.

But there were people who believed Stielow was innocent. A women's group opposed to capital punishment managed to have his execution postponed several times. One reprieve from the governor came after Stielow was already strapped into the electric chair.

Then a breakthrough came. A criminal already serving time in prison on other charges confessed that he and an accomplice had killed Phelps and robbed his house while passing through West Shelby. Later, under pressure from Newton and Sheriff Bartlett, the prisoner denied his confession. But the governor of New York took an interest in the case and appointed a special independent commission in the summer of 1917 to examine the evidence.

One member of the commission was Charles Waite, a quiet middle-aged worker in the state prosecutor's office. Unlike Hamilton, Waite didn't pretend to be any kind of forensics expert. He had never held a gun or looked into a microscope. Waite was convinced, however, after talking to both Stielow and the man who had confessed to the murder, that Stielow was innocent, and he was prepared to do whatever he could to prove it.

Waite found a gun expert on the police force and had him examine Stielow's revolver. The expert looked at the buildup of rust in the gun's barrel and said he doubted it had been fired in the last three years. Then the expert fired the gun in the crime laboratory, and a flame shot back, burning a piece of paper held above the weapon. This refuted Hamilton's claim about no gases escaping from the revolver when it was fired.

Waite learned from a gunsmith that gun barrels are as different from one another as fingerprints are. Automatic cutters bore a hole into a piece of solid steel to make a gun barrel. The cutters create small ridges, called lands, and grooves. The grooves and lands form a spiral path for the bullet as it passes through the barrel and help it travel fast and straight. These spirals are different in each gun and leave their mark on the fired bullet.

Waite's expert fired Stielow's revolver into a box filled with cotton and another filled with water. He then compared the bullets with those that had killed Phelps. The two sets of bullets were clearly not fired from the same weapon. The bullets from Stielow's gun were discolored, had different marks on them, and had particles of dirt from the rusty barrel. The bullets that killed Phelps were clean and were only slightly marked from the gun barrel.

Waite sent the two sets of bullets to an optical company that carefully examined them under powerful microscopes. They confirmed that the bullets were fired from different guns. This proved beyond a doubt that Stielow could not have shot Phelps. After serving three years in prison, Charles Stielow was pardoned and released.

Oddly enough, the people of Orleans County never brought the real murderer to

trial. They did not want the expense of another trial, and the case was dropped. As for Albert Hamilton, he continued to serve as an "expert witness" for some time, despite the fact that his testimony was proven wrong. Forensic science was still in its infancy. Fakes like Hamilton would unfairly tip the scales of justice for some time to come.

The Phelps murder case started Charles Waite on a crusade to perfect the scientific examination of guns in criminal cases, known today as ballistics. He spent the next three years collecting data on every kind of gun manufactured in the United States. Then he spent another year traveling in Europe, getting information on guns made there. In all, Waite collected 1,500 models of firearms. He learned how to use a microscope so he could study the barrel markings of each gun and catalog them.

Before he died in 1926, Waite had helped found the world's first Bureau of Forensic Ballistics. Thanks to him, science had a new weapon to fight crime that was as exacting as fingerprinting.

Chapter 4

Blood on the Dagger

On the evening of May 1, 1958, Marie Zumbach returned to her home in the quiet Swiss village of Plan-les-Ouates at the foot of the French Alps. She had no sooner entered the house when she heard gunshots and cries for help. Throwing open the door to her son's room, she was confronted by a tall stranger "of alarming appearance." She fled from the assailant and was shot in the shoulder. The man briefly ran back into her son's room. Then he tore out of the house, making his escape on a bicycle. Mrs. Zumbach went into the bedroom and found her husband dying on the floor, shot and stabbed several times.

The motive for the murder was a mystery. Charles Zumbach, a dealer in agricultural machinery, was a quiet, unassuming man with no enemies. Although the room had been ransacked, no money had been taken. Had the murderer been after something else?

When the police questioned Zumbach's son, André, a clearer picture began to emerge. André was the musical director of a radio station in nearby Geneva. He told police he was close friends with a coworker, Linda Baud. Baud had recently broken off a long love affair with a married man, Pierre Jaccoud. André believed Jaccoud was insanely jealous of him, although he was only Baud's friend and confidant. André claimed Jaccoud had sent him several threatening letters. Had Jaccoud come to the Zumbach home to retrieve these letters? Had he killed Charles Zumbach when he was discovered by the father in his son's room?

The police were skeptical of young Zumbach's story. Pierre Jaccoud was one of Geneva's most distinguished lawyers. He was a prominent citizen with a loving wife and three children. But there were no other suspects, so the police decided they had to investigate the lead further. Detectives questioned Linda Baud. She admitted her affair with Jaccoud but couldn't believe he was capable of such a crime. Then they questioned Jaccoud himself. The lawyer did not deny the affair with Baud and even admitted he had written the letters to Zumbach. Yet he claimed all this was in the past. "I do not understand how I can be suspected in any way of this crime," he coolly told the police. Jaccoud was most convincing, but he had no reliable alibi for the night of the murder. The police reluctantly continued their investigation.

Jaccoud turned over two handguns to the police. Neither matched the bullets that had killed Zumbach. They searched his house and found a coat and a suit spotted with what could have been blood. They also found a dagger Jaccoud had bought on a trip to Morocco. These were turned over to Pierre Hegg, director of the Geneva police crime laboratory.

Hegg was an eccentric figure. He worked by himself in a tiny, poorly equipped lab that was woefully behind the times. Because Switzerland had so few serious crimes, the authorities saw little point in putting money into a modern crime lab. Hegg ran what was almost a one-man operation. Despite this, he was determined to get to the bottom of this murder.

Standard forensic tests showed that the spots on Jaccoud's coat and suit were human blood. The dagger's blade had no blood on it, but Hegg found traces of blood on the handle and in the wooden sheath. Jaccoud insisted the bloodstains were from his own blood, shed in a minor accident. To prove Jaccoud was lying, Hegg would have to show the blood came from the murder victim, Charles Zumbach.

Hegg learned from hospital records that Zumbach's blood type was O. But Jaccoud's blood type was also O. Hegg realized there was no point in trying to determine the blood type on Jaccoud's clothing. If it were O, there would be no way of telling if it were Jaccoud's own blood or the victim's blood. If the blood type were not O, it could have no bearing on the case.

Hegg, however, had no intention of giving up. He turned for help to Dr. Erik Undritz, a respected hematologist—a scientist who studies blood. Unlike Hegg, Undritz had no experience in forensic science and had never before been involved in a criminal case.

Undritz took samples of the dried blood and stained them with chemicals to study the structure of their cells. As he examined the blood cells under his microscope, he suddenly noticed something startling—larger structures that he called "tissue fragments of an internal organ." Further tests showed these fragments to be liver cells.

When he told Hegg what he had found, Hegg became excited. He told Undritz that one of the stab wounds had punctured Zumbach's liver. The two scientists

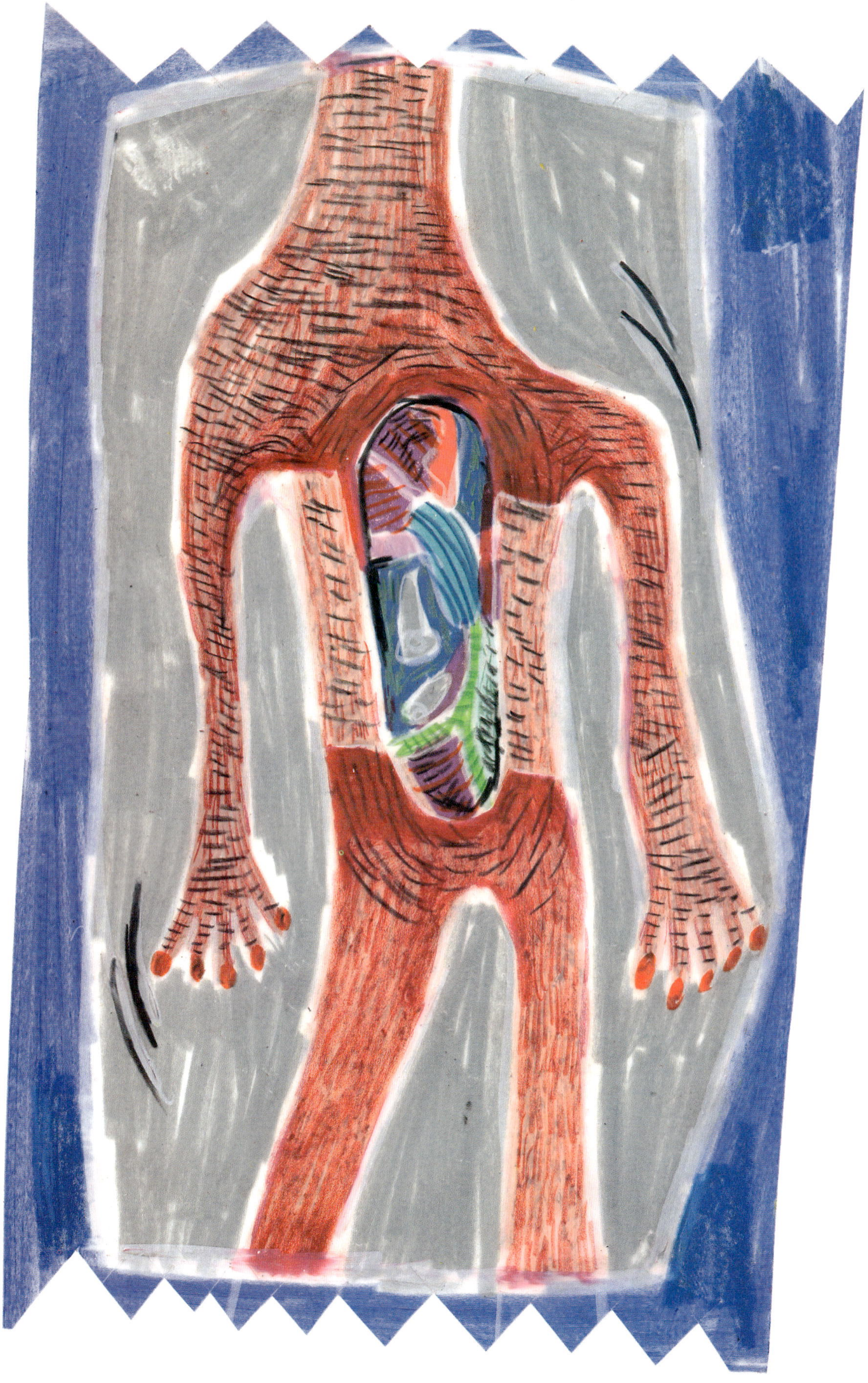

now believed they had solid proof that the dagger was the murder weapon and Jaccoud was the killer.

Undritz examined the bloodstains on Jaccoud's coat under the microscope and found similar liver cells embedded in the blood cells. Hegg developed a theory based on this evidence. After stabbing Zumbach several times, Jaccoud had put the bloodied dagger into his coat pocket. Later he probably washed the weapon, which explained why no blood was found on the blade.

Hegg knew that Undritz was a thorough and cautious scientist. He also knew that other forensic experts, both for the defense and the prosecution, would attack his findings because he was not a specialist in their field. Furthermore, the whole liver-cell discovery was entirely new to the study of blood in criminal cases and would be controversial. To strengthen their case, Hegg had Undritz further examine the bloodstains on the clothes and dagger.

Undritz used an ingenious method to figure out the age of the dried blood. By looking at different kinds of white blood cells and identifying which white blood cells were still alive in the bloodstains, Undritz was able to roughly pinpoint the age of the bloodstains. He determined they were more than a month old and less than eight months old. This meant the blood could have been shed during the murder of Charles Zumbach.

Undritz performed another test to determine if the blood came from a man or a woman. Women's blood cells have certain appendages known as drumsticks. In the blood sample from Jaccoud's clothing, Undritz found no drumsticks and reasoned the blood had probably come from a man.

All this scientific evidence—male human blood, the timetable fit, the liver cells—built up a strong case against Jaccoud. The accused lawyer was no longer a proud, indignant citizen. Although he denied any involvement in the murder, he did so with the hollow desperation of a guilty man.

When the trial began, the defense did everything it could to disqualify the blood evidence that Undritz had spent months developing. One "expert" was brought in to confuse the jury and then conveniently leave to catch a plane before the prosecution could question him. The plan failed when the judge ordered the expert to stay. The man then tried to discredit Undritz's blood slides by comparing them to better ones in a science book. The slides in the book, it turned out, had been made by Undritz!

In the end, the jury found Pierre Jaccoud guilty of manslaughter, and he was sentenced to seven years in prison.

The police believed Jaccoud had thrown away the gun he used to shoot Zumbach. If he had only gotten rid of the dagger too, he might never have been caught. But he had a certain sentimental attachment to it and unwisely kept it. That, and a few drops of blood, proved to be his undoing.

Forensic serology, the study of blood in criminal cases, has been among the most controversial areas of forensic science. In the early 1900s, blood evidence was discounted because of the difficulty in identifying blood from bloodstains and other evidence. Undritz's methods were groundbreaking and added new authority to forensic serology. By the 1960s these and other new methods in blood identification had spread to the United States and other countries. Today, forensic scientists are able to identify every individual by examining a drop of his or her blood.

Chapter 5

The Bones of a Czar

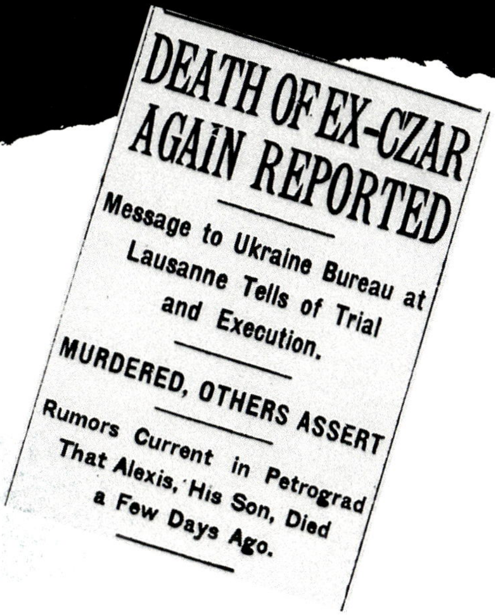
DEATH OF EX-CZAR AGAIN REPORTED

Message to Ukraine Bureau at Lausanne Tells of Trial and Execution.

MURDERED, OTHERS ASSERT

Rumors Current in Petrograd That Alexis, His Son, Died a Few Days Ago.

The end was sudden, if not unpredictable, for the eleven Russians held prisoners in a house in a remote Siberian town, 850 miles east of Moscow. On the evening of July 16, 1918, the prisoners—six adults and five children—were herded by a dozen armed men into the building's cellar. There they were shot at point-blank range.

At least three of the adults died instantly from the hail of bullets. But four of the five children—the girls—were not so fortunate. They were protected by corsets into which precious jewels had been hidden. The executioners had to finish off the girls by stabbing and clubbing them.

When the job was finished, the men loaded the bodies onto a truck and dumped them into an abandoned mine in a forest outside the town of Ekaterinburg. Later, they went back for them, fearing the bodies would be found. They took the bodies

to another part of the forest and threw them into a shallow pit. Then the men drenched the corpses with sulfuric acid to eat away the flesh and covered the grave with dirt and railway ties.

In that period of civil war that followed the Russian Revolution, such violence and death were everyday events as two factions—the Bolsheviks and the Mensheviks—struggled for control of the country.

The killings may not have been remarkable but the victims were. The dead were Nicholas II, last Czar of Russia, his wife, Alexandra, their children, and their personal servants. Soon after the murders, a Bolshevik commissar claimed, "The world will never know what we did with them." He was right—until 1979.

That year, Galy Ryabov, a Soviet crime writer and former policeman, discovered the burial pit and the remains of the royal family. He kept his remarkable discovery a secret for ten years. Why? He said the Communist government of the Soviet Union did not want the whereabouts of the czar that their revolution had over-

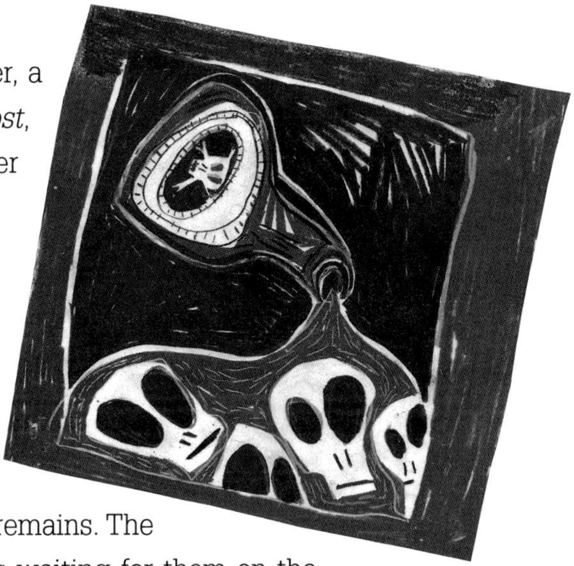

thrown to be revealed. By 1989, however, a new policy of openness, called *glasnost,* allowed the truth to be revealed after decades of censorship.

Still, the government moved slowly, and it was another two years before the remains in the pit outside Ekaterinburg were officially unearthed. In August of 1991, a team of forensic experts from Moscow arrived in Ekaterinburg to begin the difficult task of identifying the remains. The experts found heaps and heaps of bones waiting for them on the floor of the local police station.

For over three months, the forensic team put together more than seven hundred bones and bone fragments to form nine skeletons—five female and four male. There was little doubt that the people had met a violent end. There were bullet holes in skulls and crushed and broken bones. But what solid proof did they find that these were the remains of Russia's last royal family?

First, the bodies, unlike other skeletons found in the area, were hidden, as if there were some reason the killers did not want them found. Second, five of the people, according to the experts, were "almost certainly" of the same family. Third, the "middle-aged female," thought to be the empress Alexandra, had extremely well-crafted dental work—expensive porcelain crowns—that only the very rich could afford at that time. Finally, the victims' teeth and bones were whitened and had clear etched marks, indicating acid. This matched the story of the head assassin, revealed in government files, that acid had been poured over the bodies.

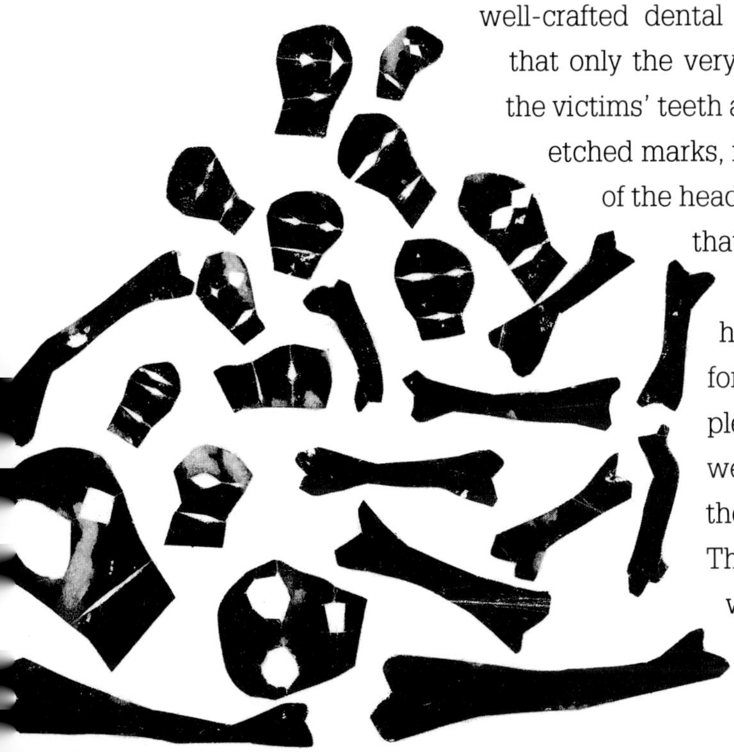

The evidence was intriguing but hardly conclusive. More accurate tests for identity, such as blood or skin samples, were impossible: all that remained were bones. Even if there were blood in the remains, it could not prove identity. The blood types of royal family members were unknown.

But there was another way to identify the remains—a new, innovative forensic process called DNA fingerprinting. This new means of identification was still controversial and not in general use in Russia or many other countries. Great Britain was the leader in DNA fingerprinting, the process having been developed by molecular biologists there in the early 1980s.

The DNA (deoxyribonucleic acid) molecule carries the genetic code that determines a person's physical and mental characteristics. It is unique to each individual, much as fingerprints are. Forensic scientists can extract the DNA molecule from skin tissue, bone, dried blood, or even a single hair. They can then compare it with the DNA of an accused person or victim for positive identification.

A tentative identification of the Russian bones was made by the Russians and a visiting team of United States experts. Then, in September of 1992, nine femur bones—one from the thigh of each skeleton—were sent off to the British Home Office's forensic research center in Berkshire, England, for further genetic testing.

The English team first did a conventional DNA analysis. Then the DNA molecules taken from each skeleton were compared to each other, to see if similarities pointed to a family relationship. They did with the five people thought to be members of the royal family—two adults and three children. The DNA in a certain part of the children's cells were exact replicas of the DNA molecules of the mother, as they should be, since this kind of DNA is only inherited from the mother. The five were then compared with DNA extracted from locks of hair of the royal family kept in the Museum of the October Revolution. As further proof, the DNA fingerprints from the remains were compared with those taken from hair and blood samples given by living descendants of both Nicholas's and Alexandra's families, including Prince Philip of England.

In each case, the DNA fingerprints matched or were similar. On July 9, 1993, the British forensic team announced that the remains from the Ekaterinburg pit were "virtually beyond doubt" the bones of Czar Nicholas and his family.

But one mystery remains. There were nine skeletons found, but supposedly eleven victims. What happened to Nicholas's son and heir, thirteen-year-old Alexei, and his seventeen-year-old sister, Anastasia? Were their corpses, as some experts believe, burned or buried in another location? Or, by some twist of fate, did they somehow survive a botched execution?

In the 1940s, a German woman, Anna Anderson, claimed she was the princess Anastasia. Some believed her story, and others found it preposterous. Anderson stuck to her story, however, until her death in the United States in 1986. Forensic experts obtained locks of Anderson's hair, and extracted DNA samples from it. They compared the samples with the DNA fingerprint of the Czar's family, but there was no match. The full story of what happened on that terrible night of July 18, 1918, may never be known.

Graveyard detection has become a serious branch of forensic science in recent years. By studying the genetic remains of famous people long dead, experts have used DNA fingerprinting to solve a number of history's riddles. A biographer's claim that U.S. President Zachary Taylor was poisoned by political enemies was proved false when Taylor's exhumed remains were tested for traces of arsenic and none were found.

The remains of Carl Weiss, alleged assassin of Louisiana governor Huey Long in 1935, showed through bullet marks on bones that he probably did not kill Long, but that the governor's own bodyguards accidentally killed him.

Other mysteries that graveyard detection may one day solve include:

- The testing of bodies found in a cemetery in Bolivia to see if they are the long-missing legendary Western outlaws Butch Cassidy and the Sundance Kid.
- The examination of the skulls of Lizzie Borden's father and stepmother to determine if the legendary ax murderess actually killed them.
- A study of the remains of Abraham Lincoln to determine if the late president suffered an inherited disease—Marfan's syndrome—that would account for his height and his unusually long arms, fingers, and toes.

As such research becomes more common, some experts are questioning its use. "The remains of the dead should be treated as sacrosanct and reexamined only for reasons of great importance," New York forensic scientist Michael Baden has said.

Chapter 6

An Almost-Perfect Murder

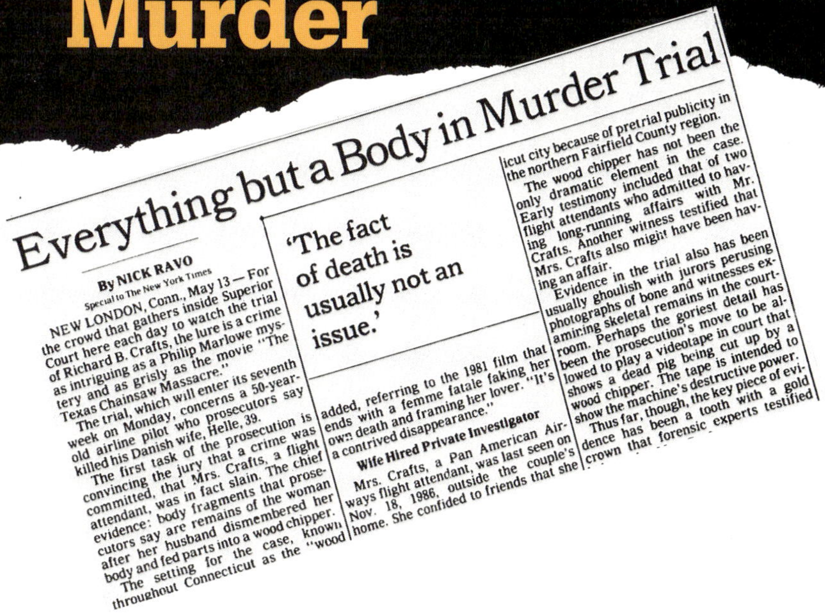

Everything but a Body in Murder Trial

By NICK RAVO
Special to The New York Times

NEW LONDON, Conn., May 13 — For the crowd that gathers inside Superior Court here each day to watch the trial of Richard B. Crafts, the lure is a crime as intriguing as a Philip Marlowe mystery and as grisly as the movie "The Texas Chainsaw Massacre."

The trial, which will enter its seventh week on Monday, concerns a 50-year-old airline pilot who prosecutors say killed his Danish wife, Helle, 39.

The first task of the prosecution is convincing the jury that a crime was committed, that Mrs. Crafts, a flight attendant, was in fact slain. The chief evidence: body fragments that prosecutors say are remains of the woman after her husband dismembered her body and fed parts into a wood chipper.

The setting for the case, known throughout Connecticut as the "wood

'The fact of death is usually not an issue.'

added, referring to the 1981 film that ends with a femme fatale faking her own death and framing her lover. "It's a contrived disappearance."

Wife Hired Private Investigator

Mrs. Crafts, a Pan American Airways flight attendant, was last seen on Nov. 18, 1986, outside the couple's home. She confided to friends that she

icut city because of pretrial publicity in the northern Fairfield County region.

The wood chipper has not been the only dramatic element in the case. Early testimony included that of two flight attendants who admitted to having long-running affairs with Mr. Crafts. Another witness testified that Mrs. Crafts also might have been having an affair.

Evidence in the trial also has been usually ghoulish with jurors perusing photographs of bone and witnesses examining skeletal remains in the courtroom. Perhaps the goriest detail has been the prosecution's move to be allowed to play a videotape in court that shows a dead pig being cut up by a wood chipper. The tape is intended to show the machine's destructive power.

Thus far, though, the key piece of evidence has been a tooth with a gold crown that forensic experts testified

Mystery writers have long written about "the perfect murder," so cleverly planned that the murderer is never caught. We have seen how a body can provide forensic scientists with many clues that can lead police to the murderer. If no body could be found, however, there would be no clues and no grounds to accuse a person of murder. This is what happened in the case of Helle Crafts, whose body was never found. And yet her murderer was brought to justice. Thanks to forensic science, the almost-perfect murder didn't succeed.

It all began during a three-day late-autumn snowstorm in November of 1986, in western Connecticut. Highway worker Joe Hine was driving his snowplow down a country road in Newtown when he saw something most peculiar. There, in the middle of the road near Lake Zoar, was a two-ton wood chipper hitched to

a parked U-Haul truck. Next to the chipper was a man in an orange poncho who gestured him to go around.

Hine did so but later couldn't get the incident out of his mind. What was someone doing out in the middle of a snowstorm on a back road with a wood chipper? The snowplow driver mentioned the incident to friends. Then, about a month later, he was approached by state police detectives, who were very interested in his story.

Hine took the detectives to the site where he had seen the man and the wood chipper. The detectives examined the area carefully. In a frozen pile of wood chips they found some address stickers and a torn envelope with the name "Helle Crafts" on it. Helle Crafts had been missing since November 18, shortly before Hine saw the wood chipper. The detectives knew they were onto something.

Two of the last people who saw thirty-nine-year-old Helle Crafts alive were fellow Pan American flight attendants who dropped her off at home early one evening. The Danish-born blond mother of three had just returned on a flight from Frankfurt, Germany.

Helle had recently discovered that her husband, Richard, an airline pilot, was having an affair with another flight attendant. Although she had asked for a divorce, Helle was afraid of her husband. "If something happens to me, please don't assume it was an accident," she told her friends.

When Helle didn't show up for work for several days, her friends were concerned and called her home. Richard Crafts told them his wife had flown unexpectedly to Denmark to be with her ailing mother. But one of the friends found out that Helle's mother was perfectly well and hadn't heard from her daughter in some time.

The friend contacted Helle's lawyer, who sent a private investigator, Keith Mayo, to talk to police about the woman's disappearance. "They were totally indifferent," Mayo later said. "They believed Helle was a 'stray dog' who would come home when she was good and ready." The Newtown police had their reasons for playing down the disappearance. Richard Crafts had served as an auxiliary policeman in Newtown.

But State's Attorney Walter Flanagan was not indifferent. The day after Christmas he turned the investigation over to the state police, who in turn contacted Hine. Richard Crafts, who had been home the night his wife was last seen, was their prime suspect. While Crafts was in Florida celebrating Christmas with his

children, detectives searched his home. They found spots of blood on the couple's mattress, but it could not be accurately identified. No murder weapon was found.

A few days later, police divers searched for evidence in the icy waters of Lake Zoar, near where the man with the wood chipper was seen by Hine. On the fourth day they hauled up a chain saw. The saw, along with the rented wood chipper, was traced to Crafts. On the teeth of the chain saw, forensic experts found strands of blond hair and minute bits of human tissue. State police inspector Tony Dalessio was beginning to grow uneasy. Only a short time earlier a local man had been arrested and convicted of throwing a neighbor's barking dog into a wood chipper. Had this crime inspired Crafts to get rid of his wife's body in the same grisly fashion?

Police searched the shore of the lake for more evidence. They warmed the frozen ground with kerosene lanterns to thaw it enough to dig it up and sift for evidence. They found a few more strands of hair, tiny pieces of a thumb and a big toe, two teeth, and less than an ounce of human bone fragments.

The fragments and tissue were too minute to be positively identified, but the teeth, particularly one that was gold capped, were closely examined by odontologists—forensic dental experts. They compared the teeth with Helle's dental X rays. The two matched! Helle Crafts, or at least her teeth, had been found. Richard Crafts was arrested and booked for the murder of his wife.

Over the next sixteen months State's Attorney Flanagan prepared his case. The evidence against Crafts was strong but entirely circumstantial. People had been convicted of murder before without the victim's body being found, but such a case had never been pursued in Connecticut.

The "wood chipper murder trial," as it came to be called, began in the spring of 1988. Crafts's attorneys did everything they could to weaken the case against their client. They insisted there was no hard evidence that proved Helle Crafts was dead. Expert witnesses for the defense tried to cast doubt that the two teeth found were

Helle's. The rest of the remains could not be proven to be hers, lawyers argued, and even if they were, this did not prove that Helle was dead. "A woman who speaks several languages and has extensive travel experience is certainly in a position to make herself disappear," argued defense attorney Daniel Sagarin.

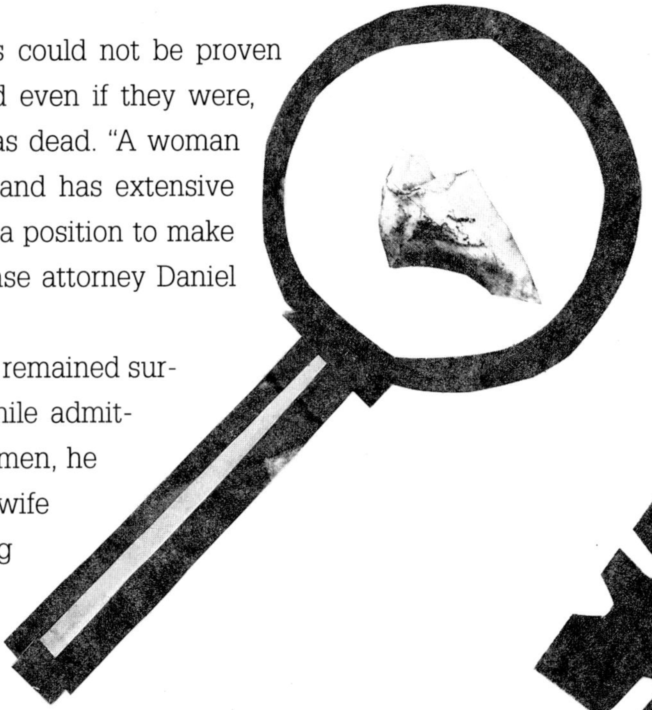

On the stand, Richard Crafts remained surprisingly cool and collected. While admitting to his affairs with other women, he held fast to his story that his wife had left home early the morning of November 19 and simply disappeared. "She was all right the last time I saw her," he claimed.

At last the two sides gave their final arguments. Prosecutor Flanagan claimed that Crafts had killed his wife the night of November 18, frozen her body in a newly purchased ice chest and cut off her head, arms, and legs—the parts that could identify her. He took the body parts to Lake Zoar the night of the snowstorm, Flanagan said, and put them through the wood chipper. Then he disposed of the torso. Flanagan called Crafts a man with "nerves of steel and ice in his veins. What other kind of person could do something like this . . . ?"

The case went to the jury. Days passed. A week. Then two weeks. Eleven jurors were convinced of Crafts's guilt. They found it inconceivable that a woman who was known as a good mother would walk out on her three young children without a word.

But there was one juror who still wasn't convinced Crafts murdered his wife. Juror Warren Maskell, a forty-seven-year-old carpenter, believed Helle Crafts might still be alive or that someone was framing Crafts with her murder. Without complete agreement, the jury could not turn in a verdict. After seventeen days, the pressure on Maskell to join the other eleven in a guilty verdict was tremendous. To end the intolerable situation, Maskell simply got up and walked out of the sequestered jury room. The judge ordered Maskell to return at once, but he refused. At that point, the judge had no choice but to declare a mistrial.

The long trial was over without a verdict, and Richard Crafts was released. But not for long. Fourteen months later, a second trial began. It was essentially a repeat of the first trial. In nine weeks the jury saw 380 exhibits and heard 115 witnesses testify. This time the jury was unanimous. In less than three days they came back with a verdict. They found Richard Crafts guilty of first degree murder.

On January 9, 1990, the fifty-four-year-old ex-pilot was sentenced to fifty years in prison. As State's Attorney Flanagan observed, Richard Crafts "accepted the challenge of the perfect crime. And he came within two-thirds of an ounce of committing it."

Although Richard Crafts failed to commit the "perfect murder," other criminals have succeeded in completely disposing of a corpse. The most notorious example in recent years is the mysterious disappearance of Jimmy Hoffa. After serving four years in prison for jury tampering, Hoffa set out to regain the presidency of the Teamsters, a very powerful labor union.

On July 30, 1975, Hoffa drove to a restaurant outside Detroit, Michigan, for a meeting with a rival Teamster leader. He was never heard from again. A car was later found that contained traces of Hoffa's blood and hair, but not enough to prove he had been killed there.

Most authorities believe Hoffa was murdered, but who did it? Where is the body? These questions remain unanswered today, but many theories exist as to Hoffa's fate. Many people think the body was disposed of in a trash compactor in Detroit. Others claim the corpse is encased in the cement foundation of Giants Stadium in New Jersey. The truth may never be known.

Chapter 7

Han van Meegeren, Master Art Forger

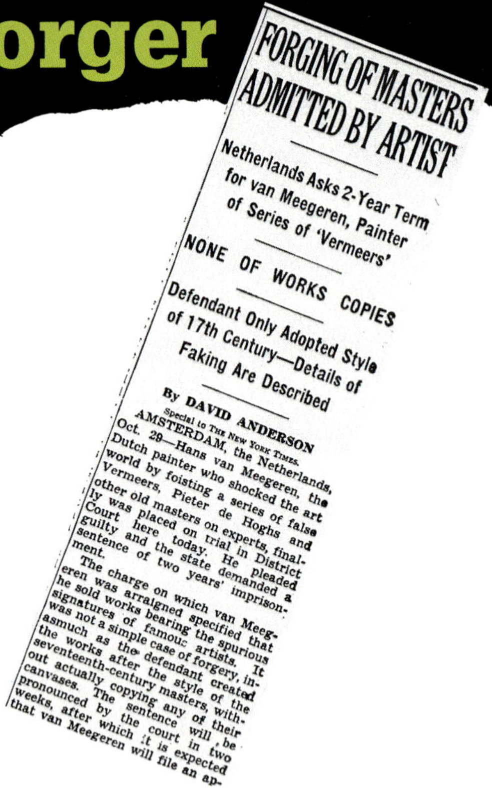

FORGING OF MASTERS ADMITTED BY ARTIST

Netherlands Asks 2-Year Term for van Meegeren, Painter of Series of 'Vermeers'

NONE OF WORKS COPIES

Defendant Only Adopted Style of 17th Century—Details of Faking Are Described

By DAVID ANDERSON

Special to THE NEW YORK TIMES.

AMSTERDAM, the Netherlands, Oct. 29—Hans van Meegeren, the Dutch painter who shocked the art world by foisting a series of false Vermeers, Pieter de Hoghs and other old masters on experts, finally was placed on trial in District Court here today. He pleaded guilty and the state demanded a sentence of two years' imprisonment.

The charge on which van Meegeren was arraigned specified that he sold works bearing the spurious signatures of famouc artists. It was not a simple case of forgery, inasmuch as the defendant created the works after the style of the seventeenth-century masters, without actually copying any of their canvases. The sentence will be pronounced by the court in two weeks, after which it is expected that van Meegeren will file an ap-

There are few cases in the history of crime in which a criminal has actually aided forensic scientists in solving a crime he committed. One of the most celebrated of these cases took place in Holland in the spring of 1945, just after the end of World War II.

When the war ended, thousands of people in Europe were arrested and charged with collaboration with the enemy—the German Nazis. The penalty for collaborating was often death. Among those arrested in Holland was a Dutch artist and art dealer, Han van Meegeren.

Van Meegeren's crime was rather unique. Three years earlier, he had sold a painting by the great seventeenth-century Dutch artist Jan Vermeer to Nazi field marshal Hermann Goering for about two million dollars. Vermeer's paintings were

a national treasure, and many Dutch people viewed van Meegeren's act as treason.

While being questioned by the authorities, van Meegeren made an incredible confession. "The picture sold to Goering was not, as you think, a Vermeer . . . but a Van Meegeren," he said. "I painted it myself."

What he sold the Nazi, van Meegeren insisted, was a forgery. When art experts expressed disbelief at his statement, he went even further. Van Meegeren claimed that a handful of early Vermeers in some of the finest Dutch museums were also forgeries that he had painted himself. The Dutch art world was stunned.

Art experts claimed that van Meegeren was lying to save himself from the

death sentence. After all, one of the paintings in question had been carefully examined by forensic art experts. The chemicals in its paints were of seventeenth-century composition. The painting's surface could not be damaged by alcohol and solvents, a clear sign its pigments had hardened with age. Finally, X rays taken of the painting revealed nothing unusual.

Van Meegeren's confession, however, raised new doubts, and the paintings had to be reexamined. The job was given to Dr. P. B. Coremans, head of the Central Laboratories of the Belgian Museums. Coremans's team of forensic scientists went to work at once, reexamining the paintings.

One of the telltale signs of an older painting is crackle—the network of tiny cracks that occurs when paint dries and becomes brittle. The crackle in old paintings has a certain appearance and texture that is difficult, if not impossible, to reproduce. Scientists used a long-arm binocular microscope to examine the crackle in one of the Vermeers. They found that some of the crackle was indeed old and could not have been faked. But in other areas of the canvas, the crackle did not look as genuine. X-ray photographs, called radiographs, revealed that these cracks did not penetrate the painting's surface.

Van Meegeren admitted that he had made these cracks by rolling his finished paintings in a metal tube. But what of the genuine crackle? How did it get there?

The answer was extraordinarily simple. Van Meegeren had taken a seventeenth-century painting by a lesser-known artist and scraped off most of the paint. Then he had painted his fake Vermeer over it, while being extremely careful not to destroy the crackle. In one painting, *Christ and the Disciples at Emmaus,* van Meegeren ran into a problem. One patch of white paint from the original painting refused to come off. The forger cleverly painted a tablecloth over the white area. Further X rays revealed a head from the original painting in the tablecloth above

Christ's left hand. This proved van Meegeren's story and possibly saved his life.

But there was other evidence to come. One forensic test to authenticate artworks examines whether the paints used are from the time period when the work was supposedly created. The presence of any synthetic paints from a later time would immediately prove the work a fake.

Microscopic examination showed diamond-shaped crystals of a pigment called cobalt blue in two of the paintings. This pigment wasn't created until the nineteenth century, well after Vermeer's time. Ironically, van Meegeren had been extremely careful in his choice of paints. He had bought an expensive ultramarine blue that was available in Vermeer's time. What van Meegeren didn't know was that the manufacturer had doctored the ultramarine with cobalt blue. The trickster had himself been tricked!

The third piece of evidence to indicate that these Vermeers were forgeries was the number of layers of paint on the canvases. In most authentic old paintings, there are three layers—the varnish, the paint itself, and the ground, or coated base surface. Scientists chipped away a minute piece of the painting and then magnified it in a photograph called a photo-macrograph. This magnified picture showed there were *five* layers to the painting, two of them added by van Meegeren to the three layers of the original painting.

While this two-year investigation was going on, van Meegeren was busy painting his last "Vermeer," to show the world how he did it. As he worked, he revealed all his technical secrets to the police. To create the look of an old painting, he used artificial resin instead of oil. This way, the paint hardened rapidly. Then he baked the canvas to further harden it. He greatly sped up a process that would normally have taken fifty years or more.

In the end, van Meegeren was cleared of the charge of collaboration with the Nazis. He was found guilty of forgery instead and sentenced to one year in prison.

Why had this gifted artist turned to crime in the first place? Van Meegeren, like some other art forgers, was seeking revenge on art critics and experts who had criticized his own original paintings. "I was determined to prove my worth as a painter by making a perfect seventeenth-century canvas," he said. To achieve this goal, he spent four painstaking years working out his techniques before he created his first "Vermeer."

Van Meegeren never served his prison term. He died of a stroke eighteen days after his sentence was passed. Although he did not achieve the greatness he desired as an artist, he is remembered as the greatest art forger of modern times.

The investigation of van Meegeren's "Vermeers" was a major breakthrough in the scientific detection of art forgeries. Both Europe and the United States have long histories of art forgery. One of the first well-known American forgers was no less a famous person than Paul Revere, patriot of the American Revolution. A gifted silversmith, Revere's engraving work was less original. He regularly copied the engravings of other men and called them his own. His most famous forgery is his picture of the Boston Massacre, which was reproduced throughout the colonies. Artist Henry Pelham accused Revere of stealing his work and giving him no credit or money for it. In a bitter letter, Pelham accused Revere of stealing from him "as truly as if you had plundered me on the highway."

Chapter 8

Death in the Sky

16 L++

THE NEW YORK TIMES, THURSDAY, JANUARY 7, 1960.

34 Are Killed on New York-Miami Flight as Plane Rips Apart in North Carolina

PLANE THAT FELL WAS A SUBSTITUTE

29 Passengers Boarded 2d of 2 Craft That Replaced a Damaged Jet Airliner

By SEYMOUR TOPPING

At New York International Airport Tuesday night, National Airlines asked 105 passengers to choose between two of its planes. No one knew it was a choice between life and death.

Four and a half hours later, twenty-nine of the 105 were dead in the wreckage of a four-engined DC-6B airliner on a field near Bolivia, N. C.

For the seventy-six others, there was a safe arrival aboard an Electra turbo-prop airliner in Miami.

Both planes were put on by the airline at the last minute, after a crack had been found in the co-pilot's windshield of one of National's Boeing 707 jet airliners.

Victims of Carolina Crash

Following is a list issued by National Airlines of the twenty-nine passengers and five crew members aboard a DC-6 B plane that crashed yesterday near Bolivia, N. C.:

Passengers

EDWARDS, Edward A., 58 years old, of 68-12 Austin Street, Forest Hills, Queens; a real estate operator.
EDWARDS, Edna, 42, his wife.
FINKLESTEIN, Mark, 27, of Philadelphia.
FINKLESTEIN, Carole, 25, his wife.
FRANK, Julian A., 33, of 28 Ellery Lane, Westport, Conn.; a lawyer with offices at 60 East Forty-second Street here.
FRIEED, Robert E., 23, of 70 Riverside Drive.
KAY, Victor H., 45, of 26 Bluebird Drive, Roslyn Heights, L. I.; an insurance broker and adjuster with offices at 55 Liberty Street here.
KAY, Ruth B., 41, his wife.
KELLER, Harry, 60, of 1308 Avenue N, Brooklyn; a knitting goods manufacturer.
KELLER, Celia, 58, his wife.
KUNIN, Leonard, of 281 Ferncliff Road, Fairfield, Conn.; manager of Kay's department

Neck, L. I. Her husband, Charles, is a certified public accountant with offices at 1440 Broadway here.
POLLO, Dr. Efren, of 10 Davenport Avenue, New Rochelle; a dentist who practiced at 1702 Lexington Avenue here.
RAMOS, Carlos, of Havana; vice president of the Continental Bank of Havana and manager of its international department.
RUBINSTEIN, Irving, about 50, Miami Beach; a haberdasher.
RUBINSTEIN, Rita, about 50, his wife.
RUIZ, Mrs. Maria, of 116 West Seventy-third Street; a machine operator in a sportswear manufacturing concern.
RYAN, James, 25, of 18 Jefferson Avenue, Rockville Centre, L. I.; a dancer with the Ballet de Cuba.
SCHINE, Gerald S., 27, of 75 Wendy Road, Trumbull, Conn.; a pharmacist in Bridgeport.
SCHINE, Jennifer, 24, his wife.
SILVER, Martin K., of 91 Ridgewood Avenue, Bridgeport, Conn.; owner of a luggage store.
SILVER, Mrs., his wife.
SWEETING, Frederick Y., 18, of 27 Madison Park Gardens, Port Washington, L. I.; a

Murray Edwards was upset. He was supposed to fly to Miami, Florida, from New York, with his wife, Elizabeth. But a crack was discovered in the windshield of their Boeing 707. National Airlines decided the plane was unsafe to fly and substituted two smaller aircraft for the Miami flight. Most of the passengers wanted to fly on the turboprop Electra, rather than the older and slower DC–6B. Unfortunately, the Edwardses got separated in the line for the Electra, and only Mr. Edwards got a seat on the plane. The last seat was taken by Julian Frank, a thirty-two-year-old lawyer from Westport, Connecticut.

When Frank saw the Edwardses' predicament, he graciously gave his seat to Mrs. Edwards and got in line for the other plane. Although the Edwardses didn't know it then, Frank had saved their lives.

Frank got aboard the DC–6B and slipped his small blue airline bag under his seat. At 11:52 P.M. that evening of January 5, 1960, the plane left New York with thirty-four people on board—twenty-nine passengers and five crew members. At 2:31 A.M., the pilot radioed to the airport tower at Wilmington, North Carolina. He let them know the flight was going well and that he was about to fly over the Atlantic to Miami. It was the last message from the DC–6B.

About fifteen minutes later, Richard Randolph, a tobacco farmer in Bolivia, North Carolina, was awakened from a sound sleep by loud rumbling. Then he heard two explosions. Randolph looked out the window and saw bright flames on the horizon. He thought about going out to investigate. But when the flames quickly faded, he went back to bed.

At 6:30 that morning, Randolph's fourteen-year-old son was on his way to feed the hogs when he saw a terrible sight—the wreckage of the DC–6B strewn across the tobacco fields. An investigative team from the CAB (Civil Aeronautics Board) Bureau of Safety was already on the way to the crash scene. When the New York flight didn't arrive in Miami, authorities pinpointed this section of North Carolina as the place where the last message was received from the plane.

It was quickly apparent from the devastation that there were no survivors. The CAB team leader, David Thompson, immediately sent several helicopters up to survey the wreckage. How the wreckage was distributed would be the investigators' first clue as to what had caused the crash.

The helicopter pilots reported that most of the wreckage was in the immediate

area of the farm. However, two large pieces of the outside of the fuselage, the plane's body, were found eighteen miles away on a beach, along with three passenger seats. What did this tell the investigators? The only explanation was that the plane had begun to come apart well before crashing in the tobacco field.

By day's end, thirty-two bodies had been found in the wreckage. Two passengers were missing; one of them was Julian Frank. Three days later, searchers found his body in a marsh on the banks of the Cape Fear River, twenty miles from the crash site.

What did Frank's body show? Both his legs had been cut off—one above the knee, the other above the ankle. The leg ends had been shredded, similar to the way they are in land-mine explosions. Forensic scientists found microscopic pieces of steel, brass, wood, wire, and blue fabric embedded in the dead man's skin. The blue fabric matched that of the canvas bag Frank was seen carrying on board the airplane before takeoff. Could there have been a bomb in the bag? It was too soon to make that assumption.

Next, Thompson had a chicken wire model of the airliner's fuselage constructed in an airplane hangar at the Wilmington Airport. Then investigators began the incredibly painstaking job of collecting and identifying the fifteen thousand pieces of wreckage and hanging each in place on the chicken-wire model. It was like completing a gigantic jigsaw puzzle.

When the model was finished, a large hole was found in the fuselage's right side. The two pieces of fuselage "skin" found eighteen miles away fit perfectly over the

Dynamite + Battery + Clock =
Boom

hole. The three passenger seats fit neatly in the interior behind the hole. From airline records, investigators discovered that Julian Frank had sat in one of these seats. It was now almost certain that Frank had been blown out of the plane at the time of the first break in the fuselage.

But investigators could not yet say for certain that a bomb had created the hole in the plane. There were several other possibilities that had to be considered first. The plane might have collided with another aircraft in the sky. Or there might have been an explosive decompression, caused by either a loosened propeller blade slashing through the fuselage or metal fatigue in the plane's structure.

As the investigation proceeded, these alternatives were eliminated. There had been no other planes in the area at the time of the crash. All the propellers had been found intact, and the hole in the fuselage was too large to be caused by metal fatigue.

To further support the bomb theory, forensic scientists turned up traces of nitrate residue and magnesium dioxide on fragments of the plane. Nitrate is a compound used in dynamite. Magnesium dioxide is found in a dry cell battery. Sometime later, investigators found a fragment of Frank's leg bone that had a piece of an alarm clock embedded in it. The three main ingredients of a homemade time bomb were accounted for—dynamite, a battery, and an alarm clock.

The team's report stated that the plane crash had most likely been the result of a bomb exploding shortly after the pilot's last message. They believed the bomb had been planted in an airline bag directly under Julian Frank's seat.

Just who had put the bomb there, and why did they want to kill Frank? Police investigation revealed that Frank had led a shady life. He was under investigation by the FBI for fraud in a number of legal cases. He had also become involved with New York's Mafia families. Frank was investing the mob's money in businesses in Las Vegas and elsewhere. Some of the investments had gone bad and Frank was in debt to the Mafia for about two million dollars.

Had the mob killed Frank in revenge, along with thirty-three innocent people? Or had Frank taken his own life to escape his mounting problems? A number of facts pointed to murder, not suicide. Although Frank was insured for about one million dollars, he did not take advantage of a double-indemnity provision on several policies that would have paid double for accidental death. If he had intended to kill himself and provide for his wife and children, why would he overlook this provision? And why would a man bent on suicide kill himself with a time bomb? A man-

ually tripped bomb would have been more reliable and far less stressful. And why take a planeload of innocent people to their deaths with him?

The insurance companies, however, accepted the suicide theory and refused to pay Frank's widow on the policies. She sued them, claiming he had been murdered, and the companies made an out-of-court settlement for an undisclosed amount of money. While the hardworking CAB investigators cleared up most of the mystery behind this bombing disaster, the final question of who planted the bomb may never be answered. Even forensic science has its limits.

After the Frank case, the public called for airlines to check passenger luggage for bombs. However, the airlines found every checking system they considered to be impracticable, and little was done. In the mid-1960s, a series of plane hijackings led the federal government to require that airlines inspect all carry-on luggage for weapons and bombs. This detection system, using metal detectors and X rays, is still in effect today. It has not, however, prevented some bombs in luggage from escaping detection in the cargo section. Such a bomb took the lives of 270 people, most of them Americans, in the Pan Am Flight 103 bombing over Lockerbie, Scotland, in 1988.

Chapter 9

The Case of the Parlor Murders

It was New Year's Eve, 1910, a night that should have marked the beginning of a happy life for a young couple in Cumberland, Maryland, who were about to be married. Instead, it was the last night of their lives.

Charles Edward Twigg broke with tradition that night and visited his bride-to-be, Grace Elosser, on the eve of their wedding. Mrs. Elosser and Grace's younger sister, May, left the couple alone in the parlor while they went about with preparations for the wedding. It was a cold winter's night, and the two lovers closed the parlor door to keep in the warmth from the wood-burning stove.

An hour passed. Mrs. Elosser went into the parlor to speak with her daughter. The two young people were still sitting on the sofa, Grace's head resting on

Charles's shoulder. It was only when Mrs. Elosser touched them that she realized they were both dead.

How did the couple die? Autopsies were performed but turned up nothing. Then doctors analyzed the contents of their stomachs and discovered traces of the deadly poison potassium cyanide. It was beginning to look like the two young people had been murdered. After his death, chewing gum had been found in Charles's mouth. Could the poison have been on the gum and transferred to Grace when Charles kissed her? If so, it was a devilishly clever murder plot.

Suspicion focused on Grace's sister May, a quiet schoolteacher. May had met Charles before her sister and had dated him for a time. Had jealousy driven May to murder on the night before her sister was to wed the man she loved?

May could have doctored one stick of the chewing gum in her sister's room

before Grace gave the pack of gum to Charles. Yet there was no hard evidence to connect May with the deaths. This didn't stop the Twigg family from accusing May of murder. The Elosser family, for their part, believed Charles was responsible for Grace's death, perhaps in a bizarre murder-suicide. Each family accused the other, and neither family attended the other's funeral.

The verdict handed in by the coroner's jury was murder by "persons unknown," but rumors continued to spread about May's involvement. Soon the young woman refused to go to school and wouldn't leave the house because she was afraid to be seen in public.

The strange deaths in Cumberland attracted nationwide attention. A reward was even offered for the person who could solve the murders. Two doctors, J. R.

Littlefield and A. H. Hawkins,
were intrigued by the case and came to town to investigate.

The doctors concluded from reading the autopsy report that the stomach analysis was worthless. They claimed that potassium cyanide is always present in the stomach in very small amounts. The doctors who had made the analysis did not note the amounts present.

Then the two doctors studied the parlor where the deaths had occurred. They learned that the Elossers had shut all the windows in the parlor because of the bitter cold that night. Littlefield and Hawkins decided to try an experiment. They brought two cats into the Elossers' parlor in a cage. They placed the cage upon the sofa and lit a fire in the stove. Then they secured the windows and left, shutting the door behind them.

When they returned two hours later, they opened the window from outside and entered the room. They found the two cats lying dead in the cage, looking as peaceful as Charles and Grace had when they were found.

The doctors believed they had discovered the culprit responsible for the deaths. It was the gas carbon monoxide. Carbon monoxide is a highly poisonous gas given off when natural gas burns. The doctors found that soot built up in the stove's vent had prevented the carbon monoxide from escaping up the flue and caused it to leak back into the room. With the windows open, the gas was dispelled by the circulating air. With the windows shut, however, the carbon monoxide built up to a dangerous level. The odorless and colorless gas had slowly put its victims to sleep—a sleep from which they never awoke.

The police accepted the doctors' findings and declared the deaths an unfortunate accident. The soot was cleaned out, and the stove was believed no longer a danger. But the vicious rumors about May Elosser continued. The family decided to sell their house and move away.

What happened next proved May's innocence beyond a doubt. Two elderly ladies bought the house and were found one night on the sofa, unconscious. Fortunately, the neighbor who found them was able to revive them before they died from carbon monoxide poisoning. The gas stove was taken apart by police. They discovered the problem was more serious than had earlier been thought. The stove's bricks were covered with soot and blocked the flue, causing the carbon monoxide to escape into the room. The case of the parlor "murders" was now fully explained, and an innocent person cleared.

Carbon monoxide kills by combining with hemoglobin, the substance that normally carries oxygen in the blood to the body's tissues. Carbon monoxide replaces this oxygen, since hemoglobin binds more strongly to carbon monoxide than to oxygen. Without oxygen, humans and animals die. Automobile engines produce carbon monoxide in large quantities. Each winter, a number of people die from carbon monoxide poisoning when their cars get stuck in the snow. They keep their motors running to stay warm in the cold, and then fall asleep. If you are ever stuck inside a car in snow or other bad weather and run the motor to stay warm, always remember to keep the window open. It could save your life!

Chapter 10

A Nose for Narcotics

Surprise, Kids! Corky Can Sniff Your Stash

A dog may be man's best friend, but some South Florida teenagers have a bone to pick with a Labrador retriever named Corky. In recent months, a number of desperate Broward County parents have turned to Corky's owner, Gene Panella, for confirmation of their worst fears: that their kids are using drugs. One mother grew suspicious when her 16-year-old son suddenly became withdrawn. After repeated denials from the boy, she paid Panella $250 for Corky to search his room. Within minutes, the retriever was excitedly clawing at a dresser drawer; inside was a sock filled with pot. A disheartening 16 of Corky's 17 searches have turned up drugs. The extremity of the parents' tactic is matched only by the ingenuity of the kids. Corky has uncovered dope stuffed into a bowling ball and tucked neatly into a slit in a carpet.

Sniffing out drugs has long been part of a dog's life—so successfully that drug lords have marked U.S. Border Patrol hounds for death in Texas. The owner of a guard-dog company, Panella began using Corky for drug searches on yachts during the federal government's controversial zero-tolerance program. On one 85-foot boat, the dog found two marijuana seeds crushed into the rug. The captain was so impressed that he asked Panella to locate his son's stash. Several entrepreneurs have approached Panella about starting similar businesses. He is training a second retriever for the drug patrol, and is willing to sell drug-sniffing dogs for $7,000 apiece. "I'm doing these kids a favor," he says. "Now they'll get the help they need."

Among the passengers entering Miami International Airport on a flight from the island of Trinidad was a man dressed in a Hawaiian shirt and dirty sneakers. Amid the bustling crowds was a sight that brought a smile to the man's lips. A few feet away, he spotted the cutest little cocker spaniel. The man's smile widened as the dog looked back at him and wagged its shaggy tail. To the man's surprise and delight, the dog circled him excitedly, as if he were its long-lost master.

Then the dog sat down right next to where the man stood. The man was about to bend down and pet the playful spaniel when he was suddenly confronted by several neatly dressed men.

"Will you please come with us, sir," said one of the men quietly. The passenger protested but accompanied them to a small room off to the side of the airport. The men identified themselves as plainclothes U.S. Customs officers and asked the man to remove his shirt and pants. The man grudgingly did so. Under his clothing the officers found plastic bags filled with the illegal drug marijuana attached to his legs and body with duct tape. How had the officers suspected the passenger was smuggling drugs?

As the officers prepared to take the man into custody for drug smuggling, he looked down and saw the dog there looking up at him. Its tail was still wagging. The man suddenly realized he'd been given away by this cute little cocker spaniel!

The drug-sniffing dog's name was Corky. He was one of the first of a new kind of police dog. Since the 1960s, U.S. Customs has used specially trained dogs to sniff out drugs coming into the country. But by the late 1980s, custom officials were finding their job becoming more difficult. More and more airline passengers, many of them unlikely suspects, were smuggling drugs into the United States. Checking each passenger's person and luggage for drugs was a challenge, especially in large metropolitan airports.

Traditional police dogs, such as German shepherds, were good at sniffing out drugs in baggage in cargo areas but were too aggressive and obvious for checking arriving passengers. So in 1988 customs officials decided to try using less aggressive, more friendly dogs to sniff out drugs. These dogs, they believed, wouldn't arouse the smugglers' suspicions.

Customs agents were sent to dog pounds and animals shelters to look for likely recruits. A good nose was not the most important requirement, although many dogs have an extraordinary sense of smell. Agents were looking for dogs that were intelligent, liked people, and wanted to please them. These dogs could be easily trained and would work tirelessly for their trainers.

Corky, the cocker spaniel, was found in an animal shelter in Peoria, Illinois. He fetched the ball the officer threw him and responded enthusiastically to his words of praise. Corky was sent to the Detector Dog Training Center Academy in Front Royal, Virginia. There, he went through an intense ten-week training program with

his new partner, Canine Enforcement officer Ricky Grim. In the first week of training Ricky threw Corky a rolled towel scented with different drugs. Ricky praised Corky every time he picked up the towel. Within days, Corky became extremely familiar with the smell of each drug. Cocaine had a dull, metallic smell. Heroin smelled like vinegar and marijuana like wild herbs.

The second week Ricky began hiding the rolled drug-scented towels inside boxes, suitcases, and carry-on bags. The towels were even hidden on the bodies of staff volunteers. Each time, Corky was able to sniff out the drugs. Ricky taught the dog to lie down next to the person or object that contained the drugs. This was the signal for Ricky and custom officials to move in and search the suspect or the object.

When the ten weeks were over, Corky and Ricky were ready to go to work. They were assigned to Miami International Airport. On his very first day on the job, Corky proved his training wasn't wasted. While cruising a line of passengers disembarking from a flight from Trinidad, he picked out an attractive woman in a purple dress. Officers later found several vials of liquid cocaine on her body.

Corky's nose for narcotics wasn't fooled by other smells meant to throw him off the scent. One time, he sniffed drugs in a cooler full of seafood. As the cooler's owner went through customs, officers put a hole in the side of the cooler. They found seven pounds of cocaine packed inside the lining. The man was furious and vented his anger on the dog who turned him in. He lashed out and kicked poor Corky.

Not all the people caught by Corky have been so vengeful. One smuggler stepped off a flight from Bolivia carrying a Bible and five and a half pounds of cocaine. When he was caught with Corky's help, he showed no hard feelings toward the dog. He even asked that his picture be taken with Corky in his lap!

Corky's sense of smell was so keen that he could detect the smell of drugs on other objects that had come in contact with them. One time he lay down alongside a well-dressed man, who was then searched by custom officers. They found no drugs on the man, but did find $21,000 in cash in his jacket pocket. A residue of cocaine was found on the bills. Officers concluded that the money had been part of a recent drug deal. Since no drugs were found, the man was arrested for bringing undeclared currency into the country.

By the end of his first year working for customs, Corky had found more than 300 pounds of marijuana, more than 150 pounds of cocaine, and $57,000 in undeclared money at the Miami Airport.

The use of drug-sniffing pet dogs, including cocker spaniels and golden retrievers, was a resounding success. The program has been expanded to airports in other large cities—Houston, Los Angeles, Chicago, and New York City. A nose for narcotics has made man's best friend the drug smuggler's worst enemy.

Drugs are not the only things that police dogs have been trained to sniff out. During the Prohibition Era (1920–1933), the manufacture and sale of alcoholic beverages was illegal in the United States. Dogs were used to sniff out "moonshiners" and their whiskey stills. In more recent years, dogs have been used successfully to sniff out bombs and explosives.

But dogs aren't the only animals used in this kind of detective work. The U.S. Embassy in Colombo, Sri Lanka, has conducted a training school for drug-sniffing mongooses—furry mammals with a remarkable sense of smell found in Asia and Africa. Unlike dogs, mongooses don't tire easily in the intense heat of those continents, and they don't offend native Muslim peoples, who believe dogs to be unclean animals.

Index

Photo and Article Credits

page 15: UPI/Bettmann; page 21: *The New York Times*, April 24, 1915, p. 7; page 27: Superstock; page 33: *The New York Times*, June 28, 1918, p. 1; page 39: *The New York Times*, May 15, 1988, sec. 1, p. 28; page 46: *The New York Times*, October 30, 1947, p. 27; page 53: *The New York Times*, January 7, 1960, p. 16; page 62, The New York Public Library Picture Collection; page 68: *Newsweek*, August 8, 1988, p. 33.